I am fishing in a river.
I have a fishing rod
and line.

Little Rascals Preschool
P.O. Box 1162
Kalama, WA 98625

1

There is a hook on the line.
There is a worm on the hook.
The worm is bait.

2

A fish can swim to the bait.
It does not see the hook.
It bites the bait on the hook.

3

The hook is in the fish's mouth.
The fish is pulling the line.
The float goes down.
I pull the line in.
4

The fish cannot breathe on land.
It can only live in water.
It will die on land.

Mummy fries our fish.
She fries them in oil.
They will be good to eat.
6

Many fish are good to eat.
This shop sells fish.
Most of them come
from the sea.

The fishing boat is at sea.
Fishermen are catching fish with nets.
They catch them to sell.

8

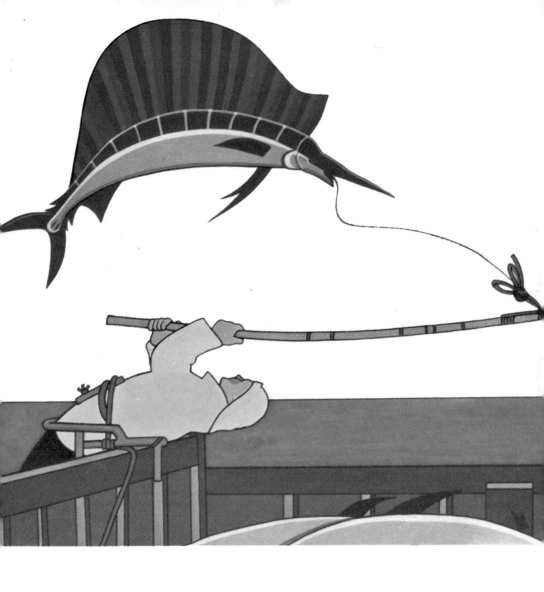

This man catches a big
sail fish on his line.
It jumps high in the air.

This salmon can jump high.
It jumps up
a little waterfall.

10

Flying fish glide a long way.
They have big fins.
The fins help them glide.

11

Sharks have very sharp teeth.
They catch other fish to eat.

12

This is a hammerhead shark.
Its head has a shape like a hammer.

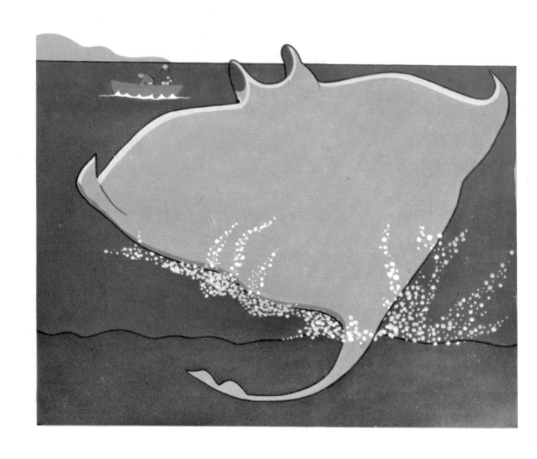

This big fish is a ray.
It jumps right out of the water.
Some people call it the Devil Fish.
14

This fish has a long spike on its nose.
It is called a sword fish.

15

This is an angler fish.
It has a fishing rod on its nose.
There is a light on the end.
Little fish swim into his mouth.

16

All these fish live in very deep water.
Deep water is dark.
Many of the fishes make light.

These are tropical fish.
They live in warm water.
Many have bright colours.

18

Puffer fish live in warm water.
They can puff themselves up
like balloons.

These fish are flat-fish.
Most flat-fishes can change colour.
This helps them hide.
20

These fish are sea-horses.
They are tiny.
They have heads like horses.

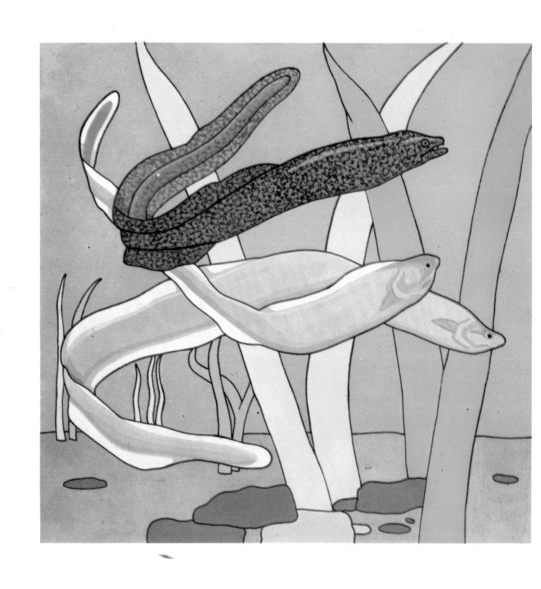

These fish are eels.
Most eels look like snakes.

22

Starter's **Fish** words

fishing
(page 1)

bait
(page 2)

float
(page 1)

fry
(page 6)

fishing rod
(page 1)

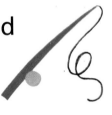

shop
(page 7)

line
(page 1)

fishing boat
(page 8)

hook
(page 2)

fisherman
(page 8)

net
(page 8)

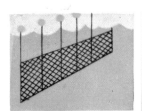

flying fish
(page 11)

sail fish
(page 9)

fin
(page 11)

salmon
(page 10)

shark
(page 12)

jump
(page 10)

teeth
(page 12)

waterfall
(page 10)

hammerhead shark
(page 13)